I0416660

For all those who believe that the study of history is a powerful key to interpreting our society.

Waldy Lau Filho
2024

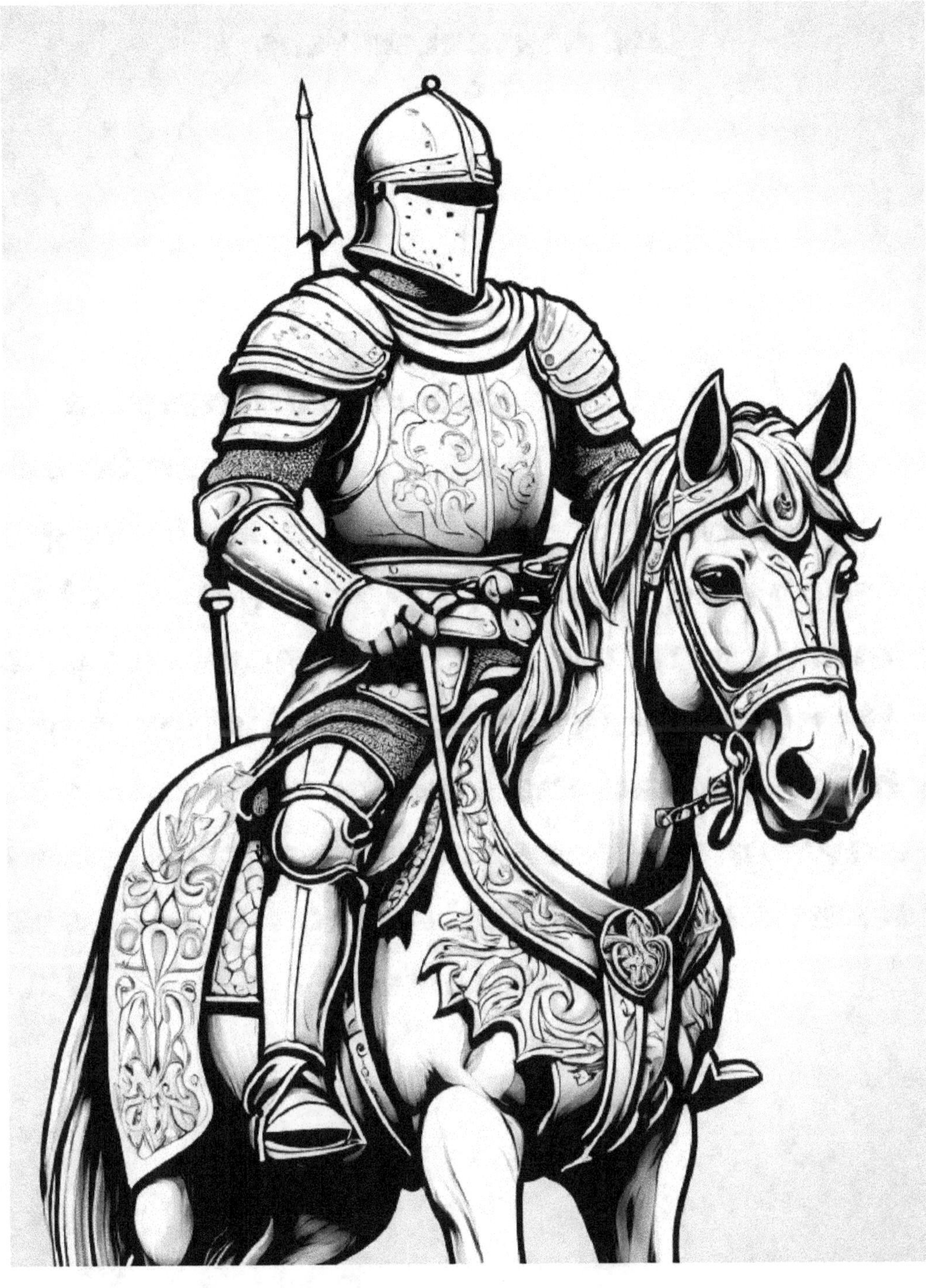

This historical coloring book belongs to:

WLF©

WALDY'S HISTORICAL PUBLICATIONS

Test color page

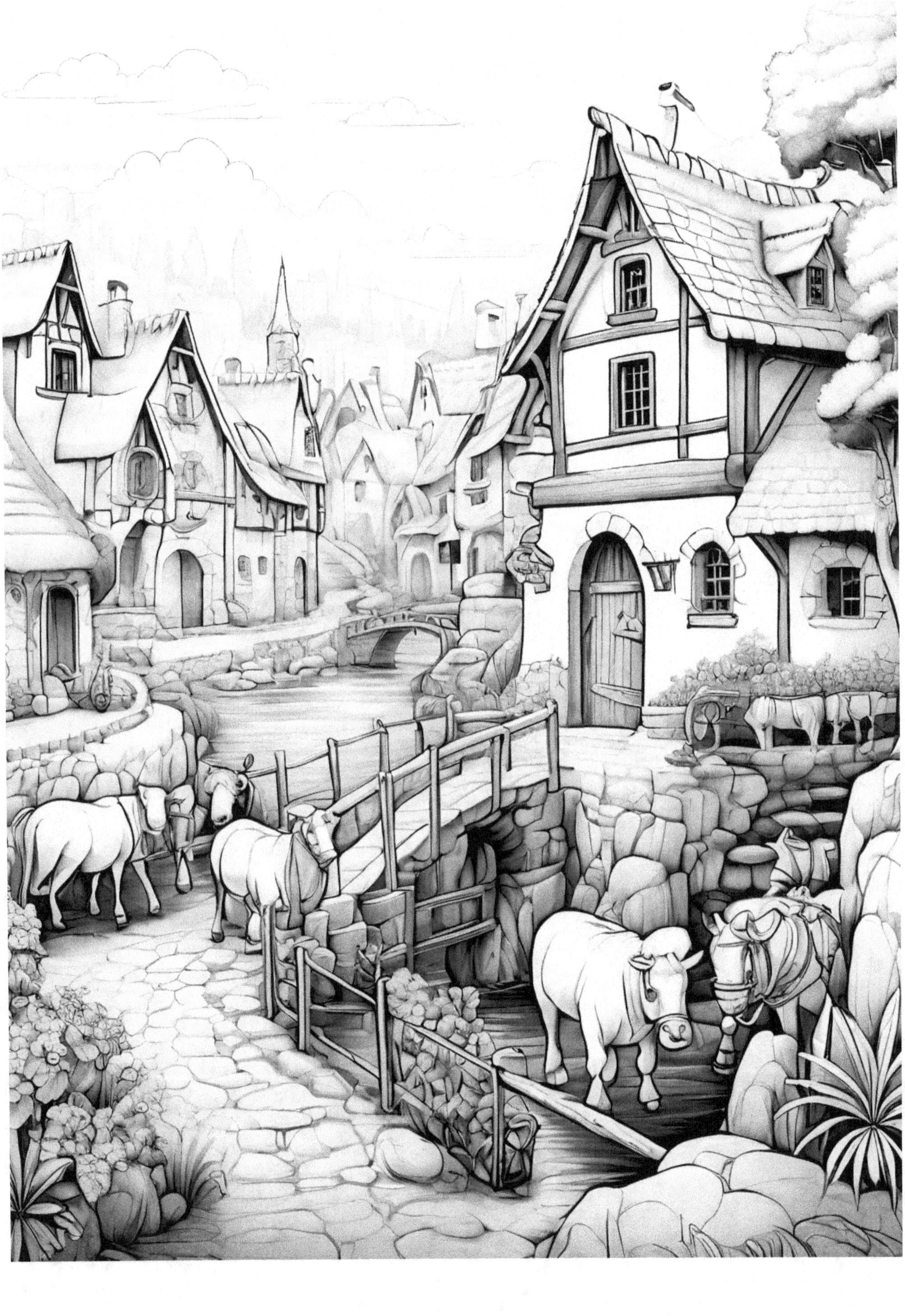

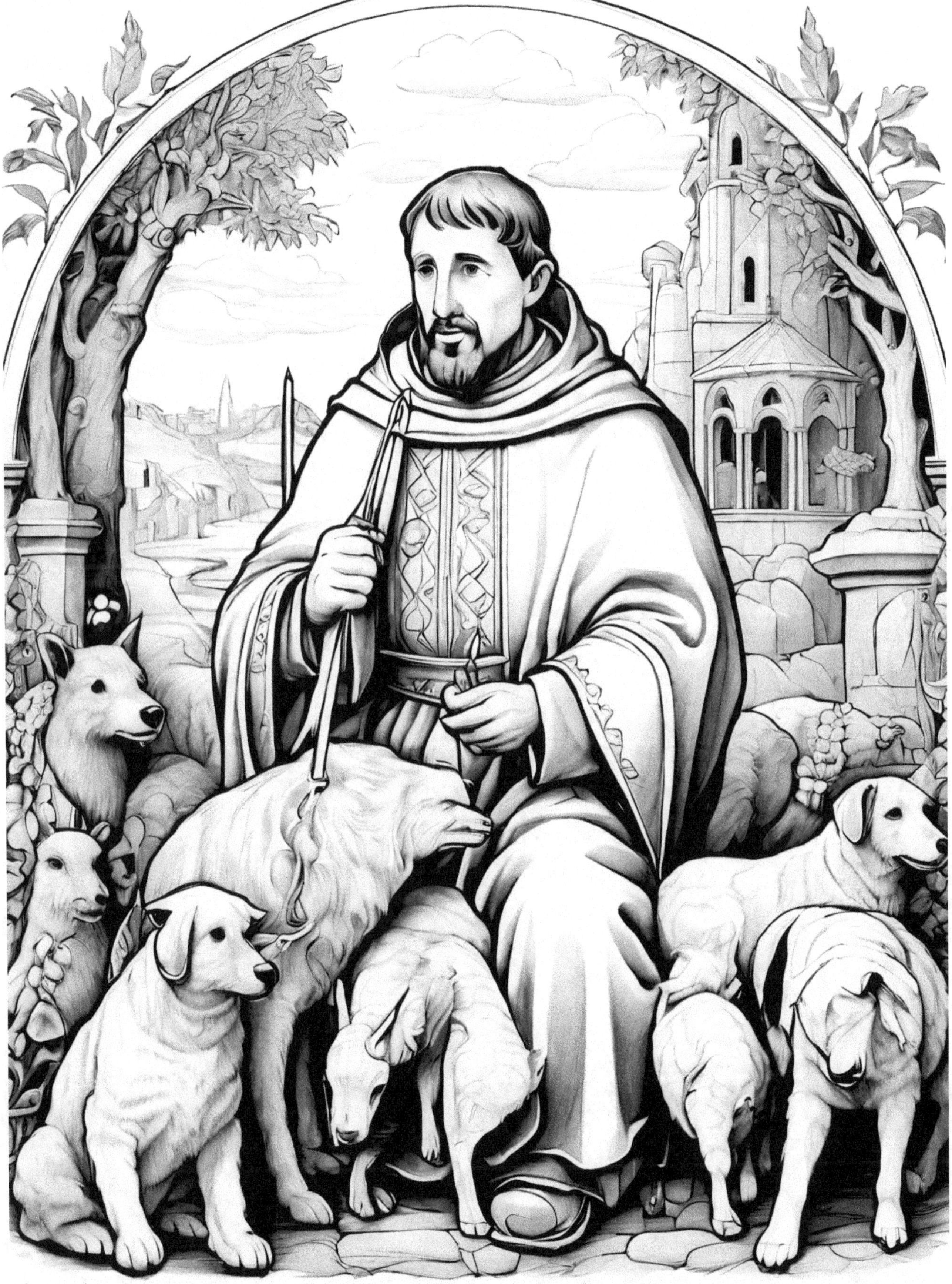

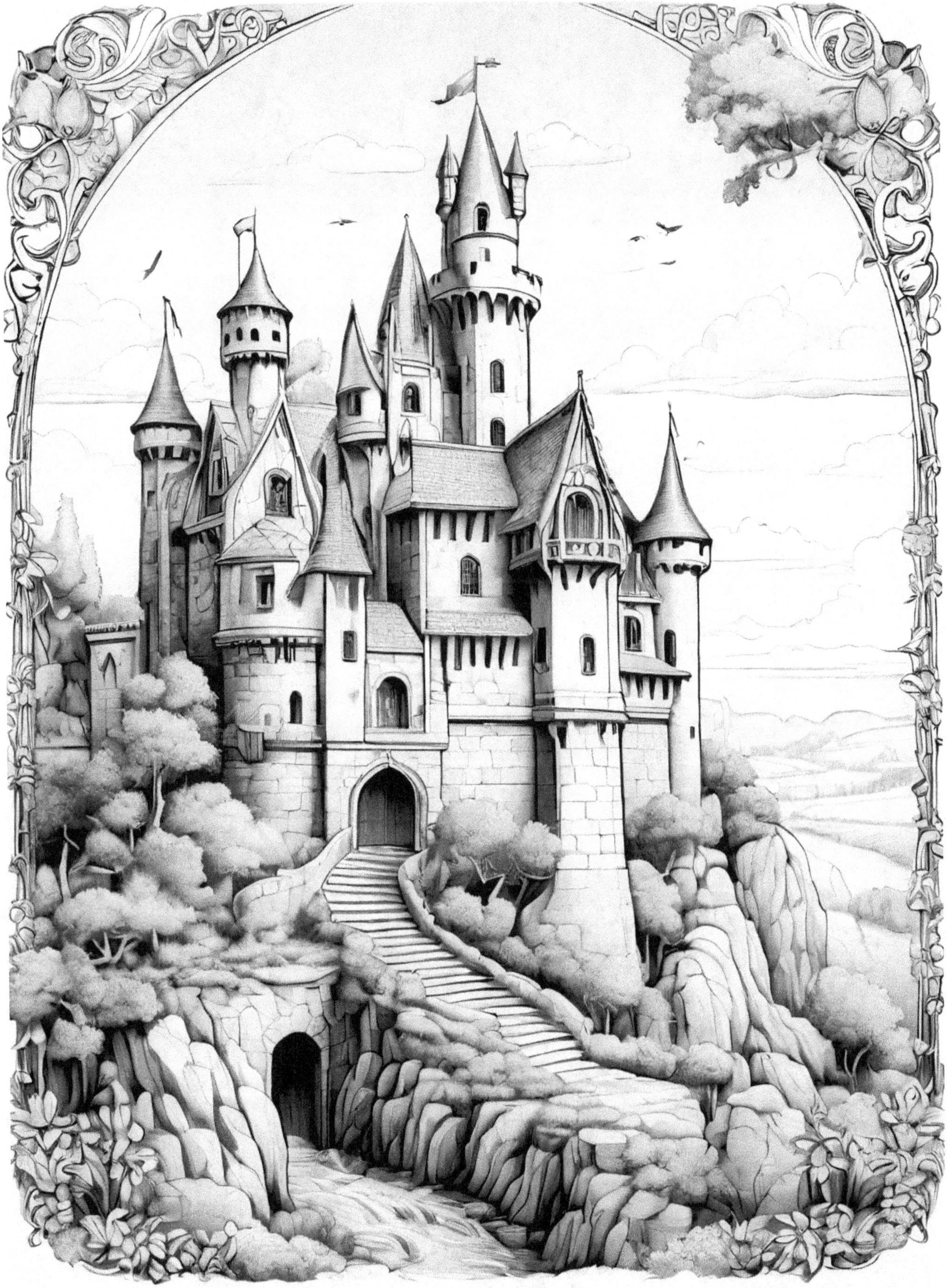

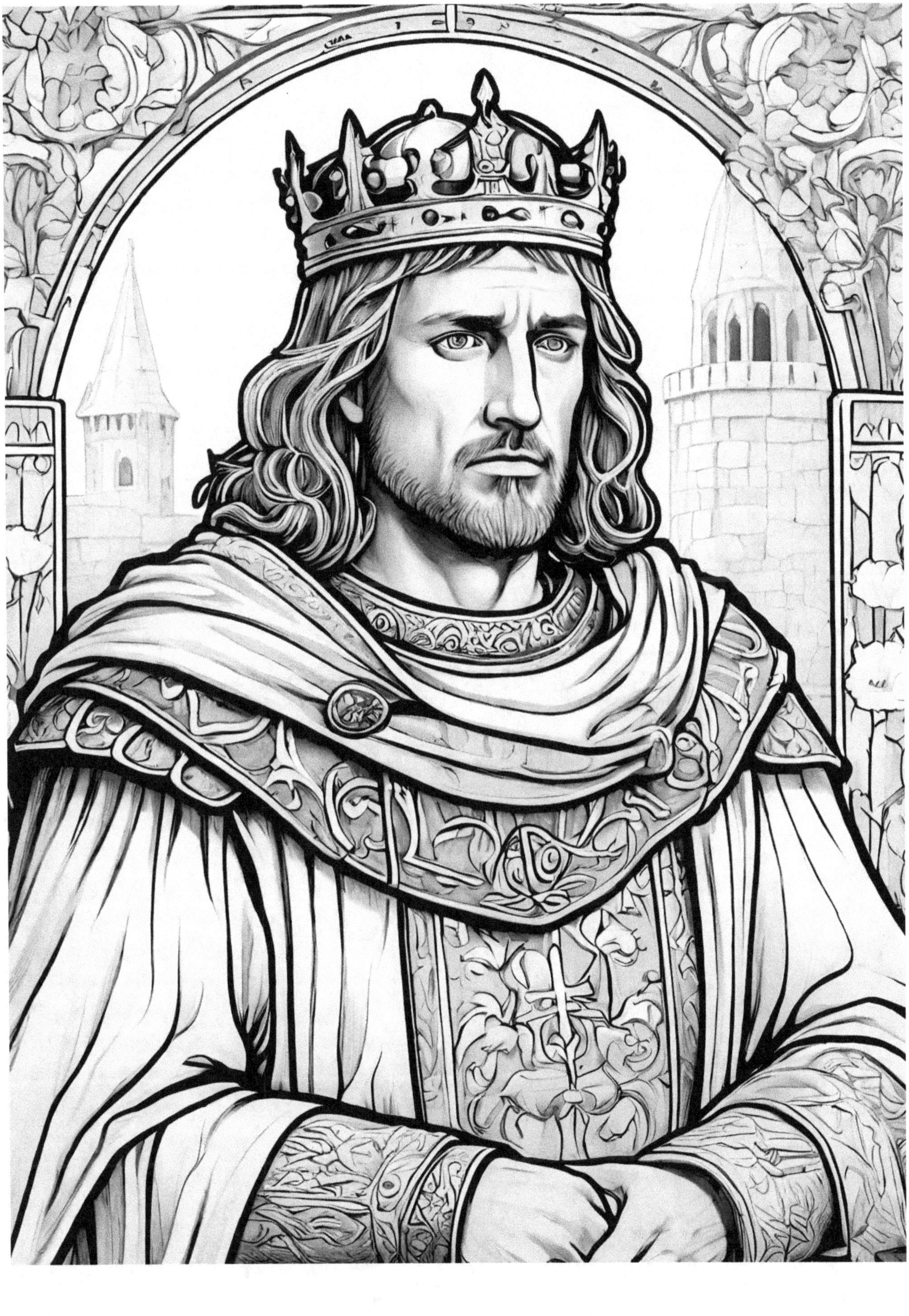

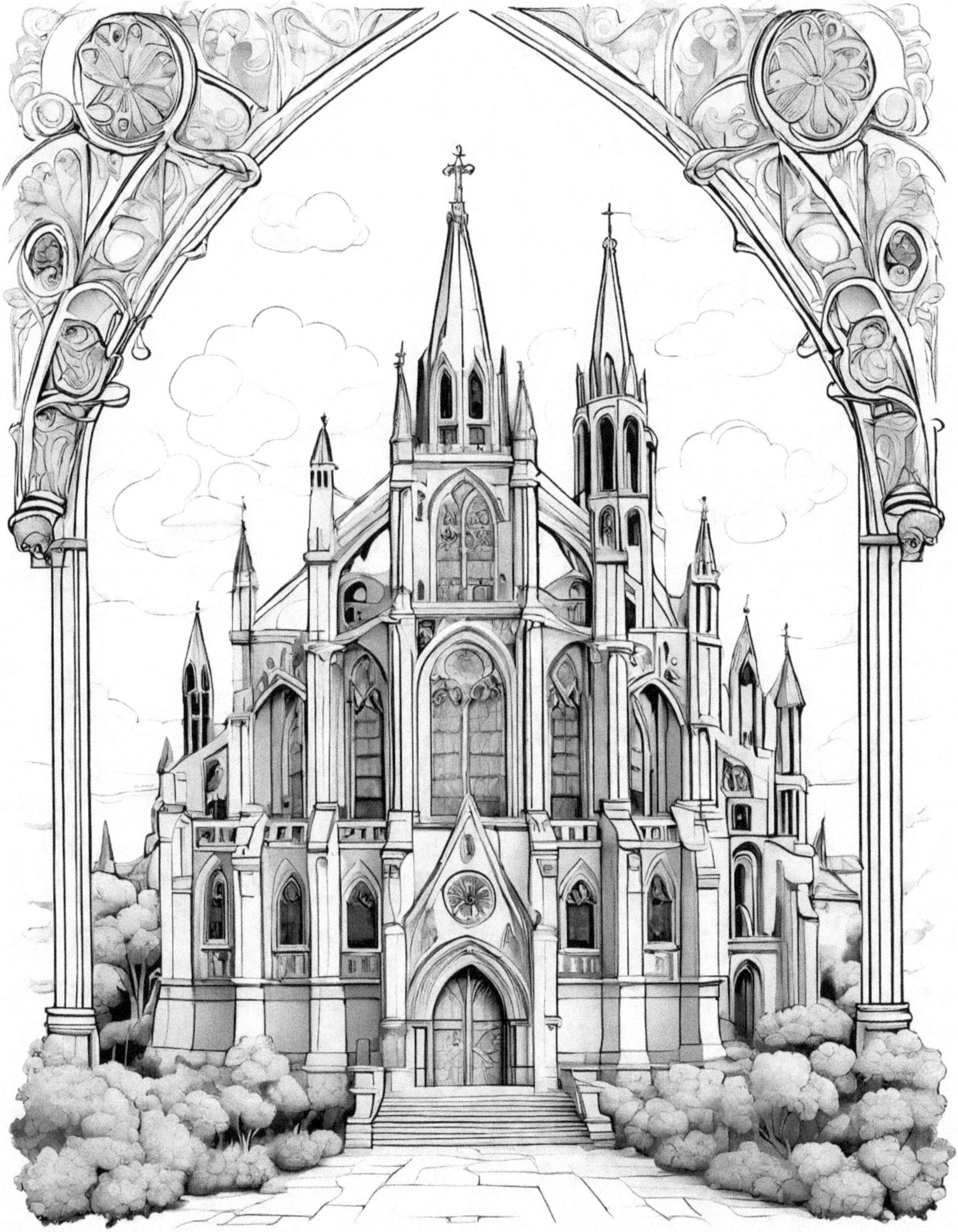

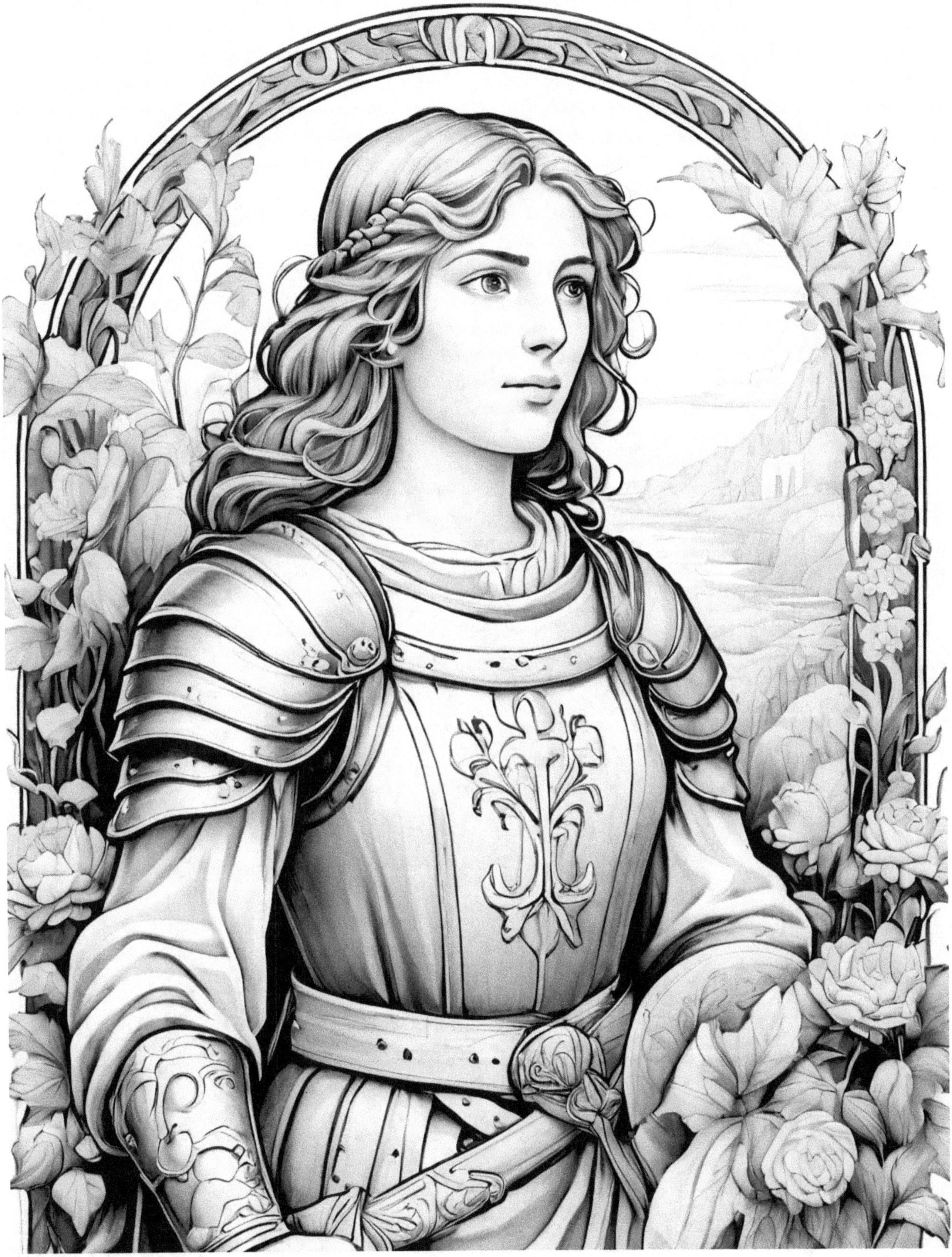

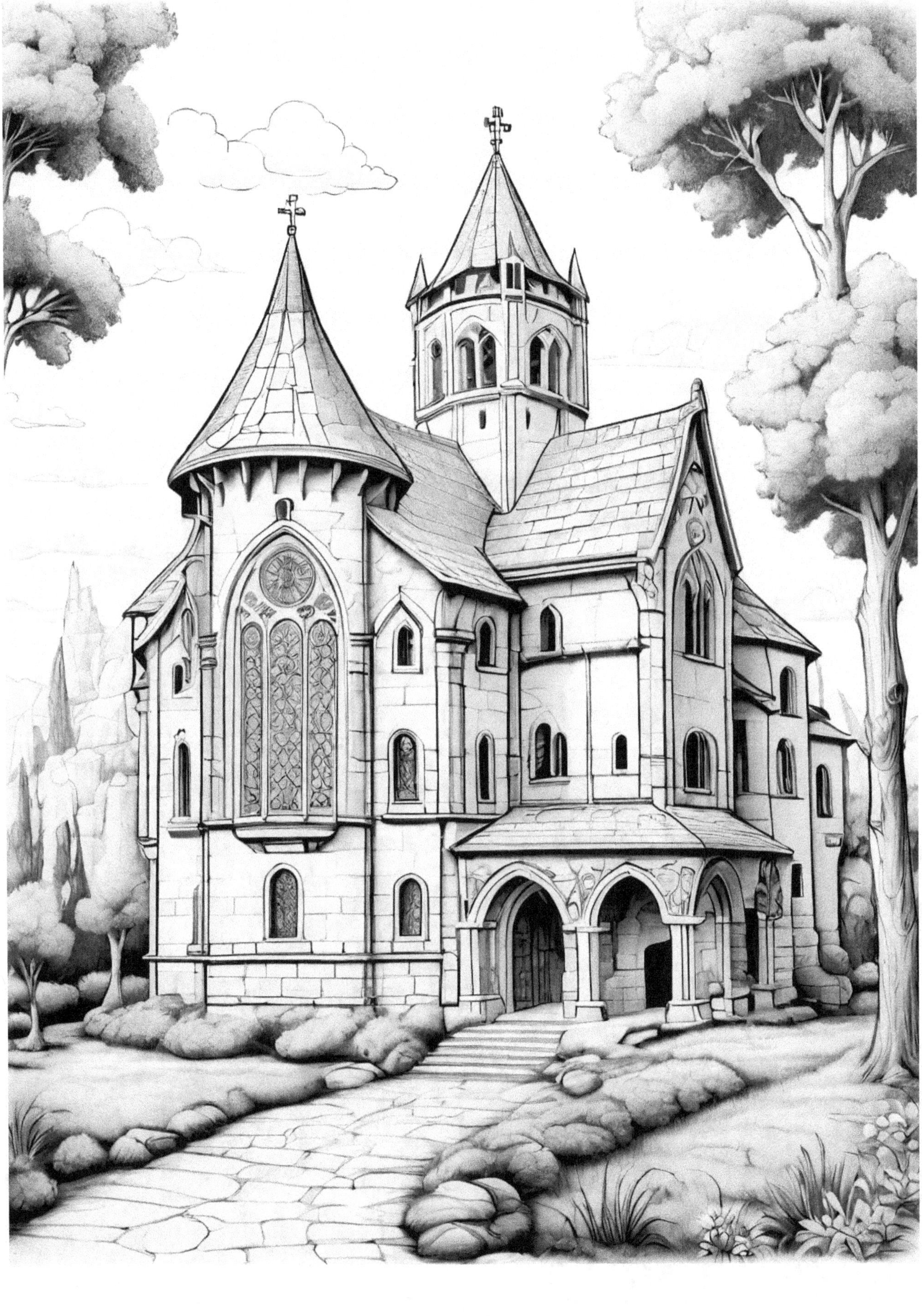

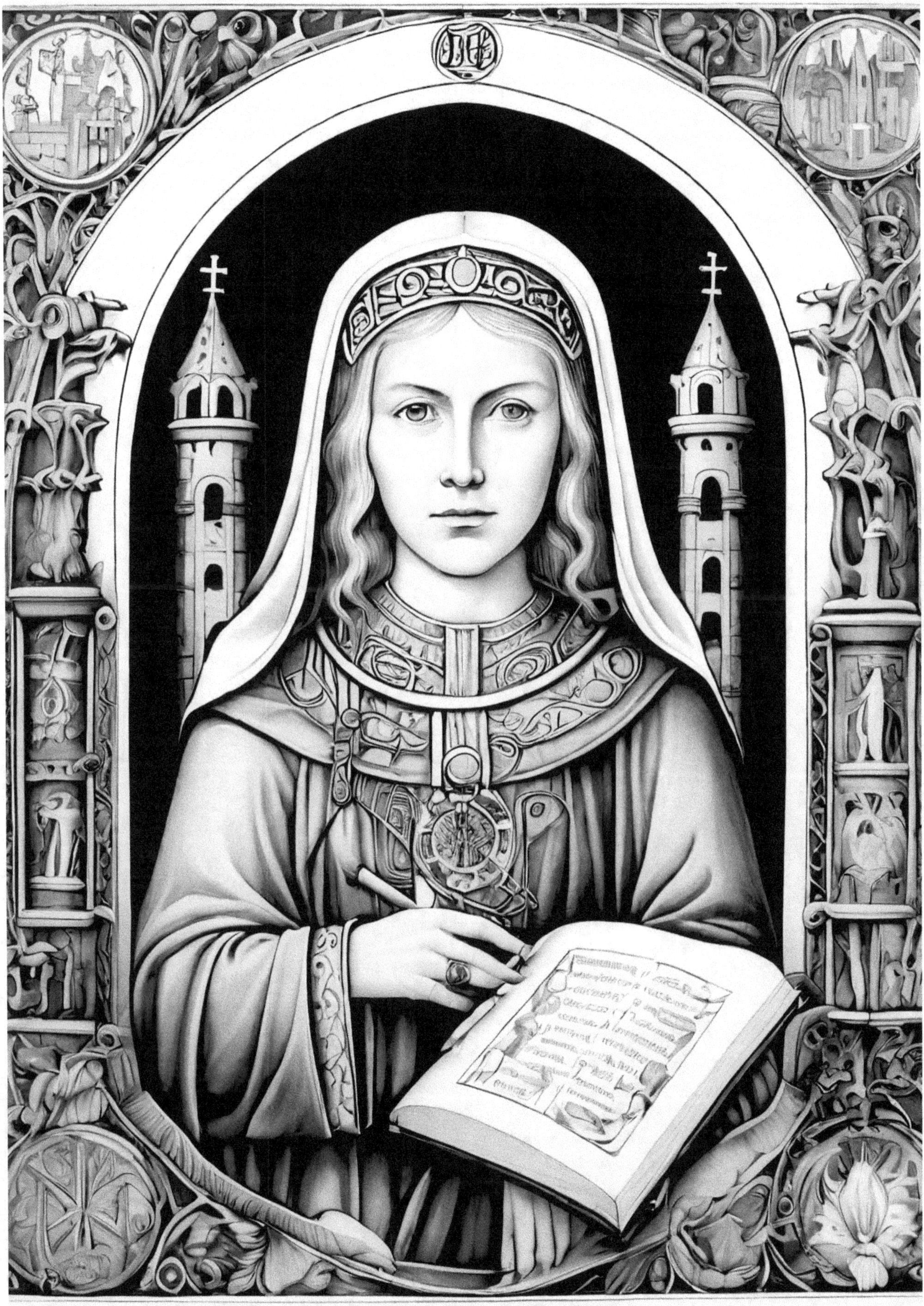

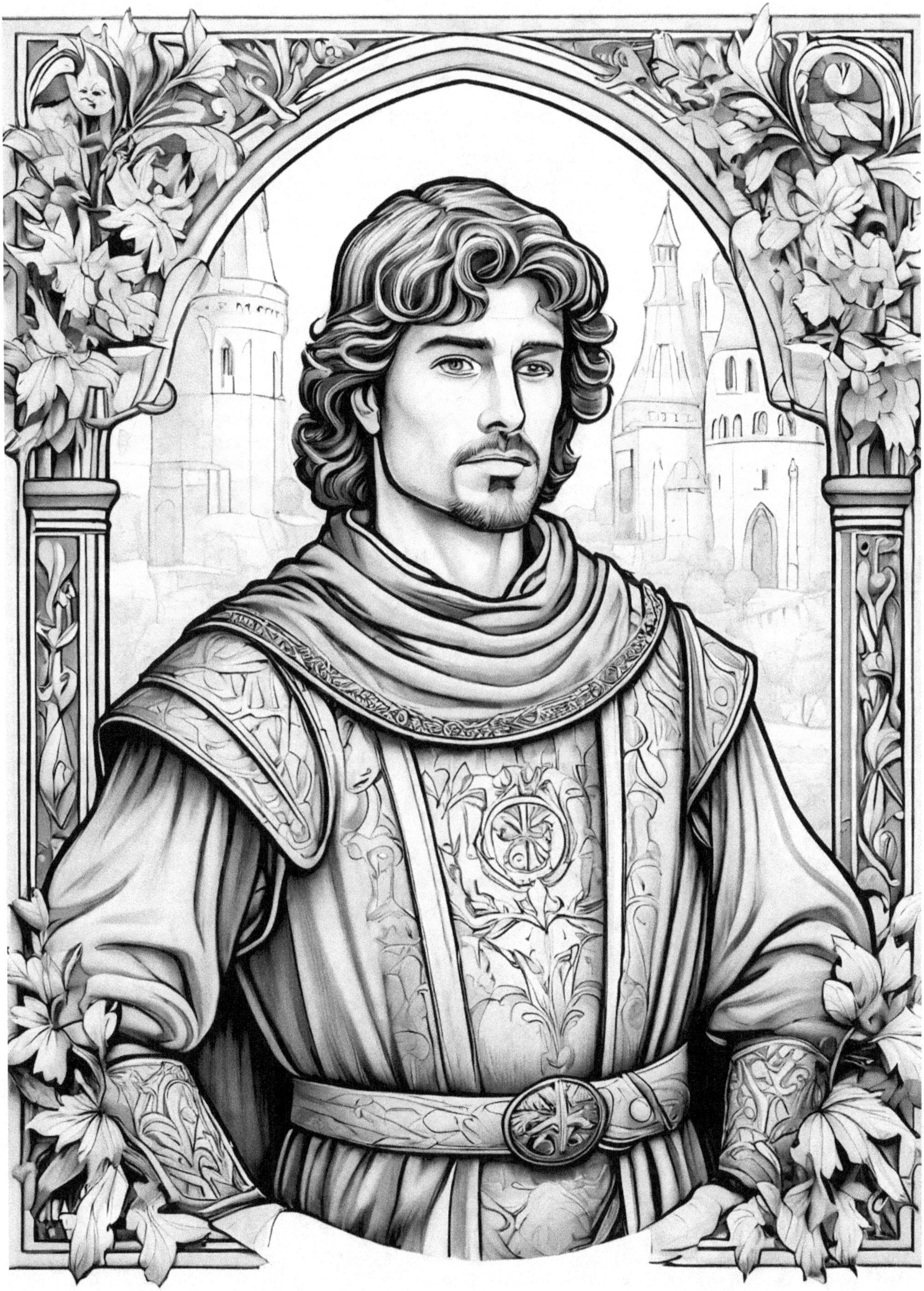

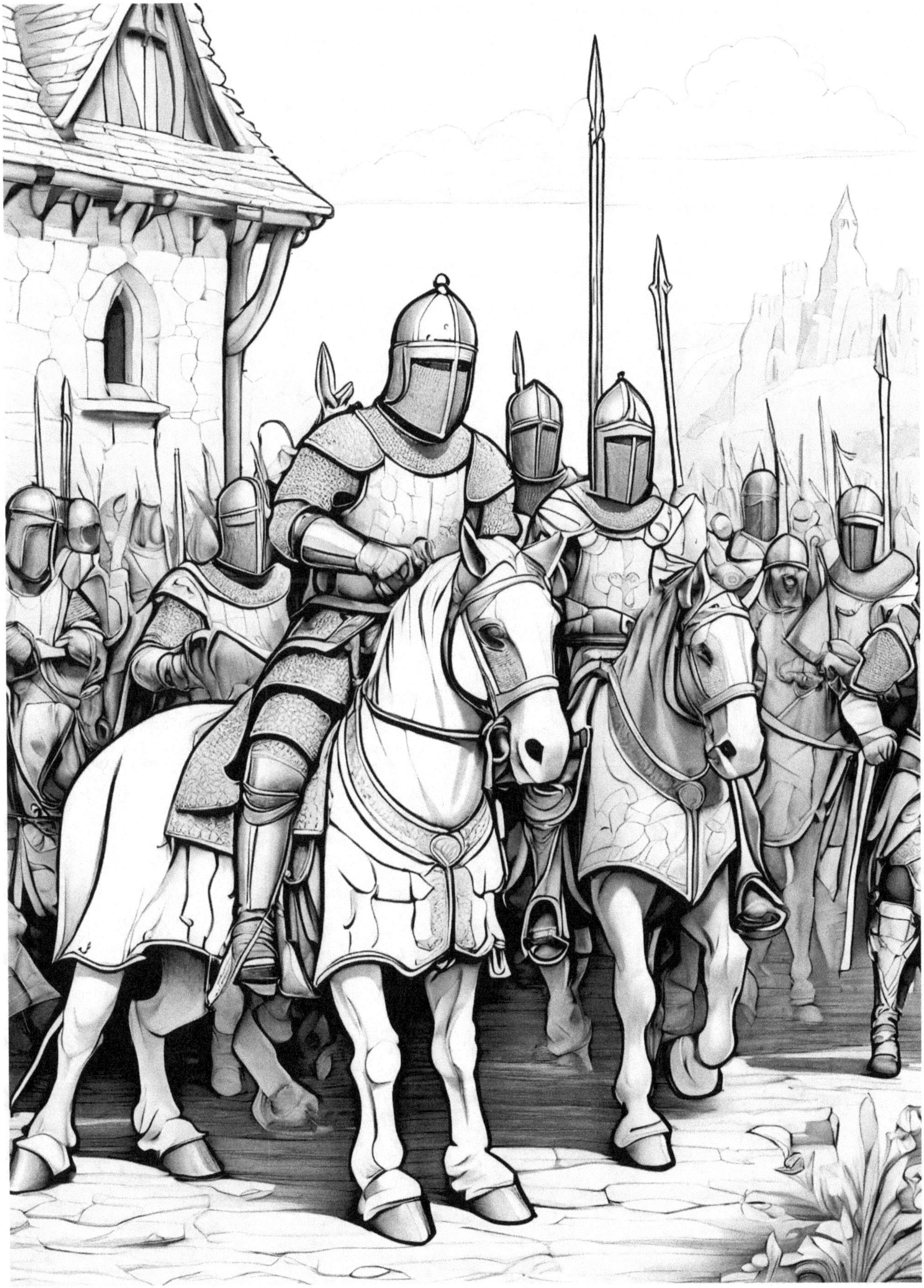

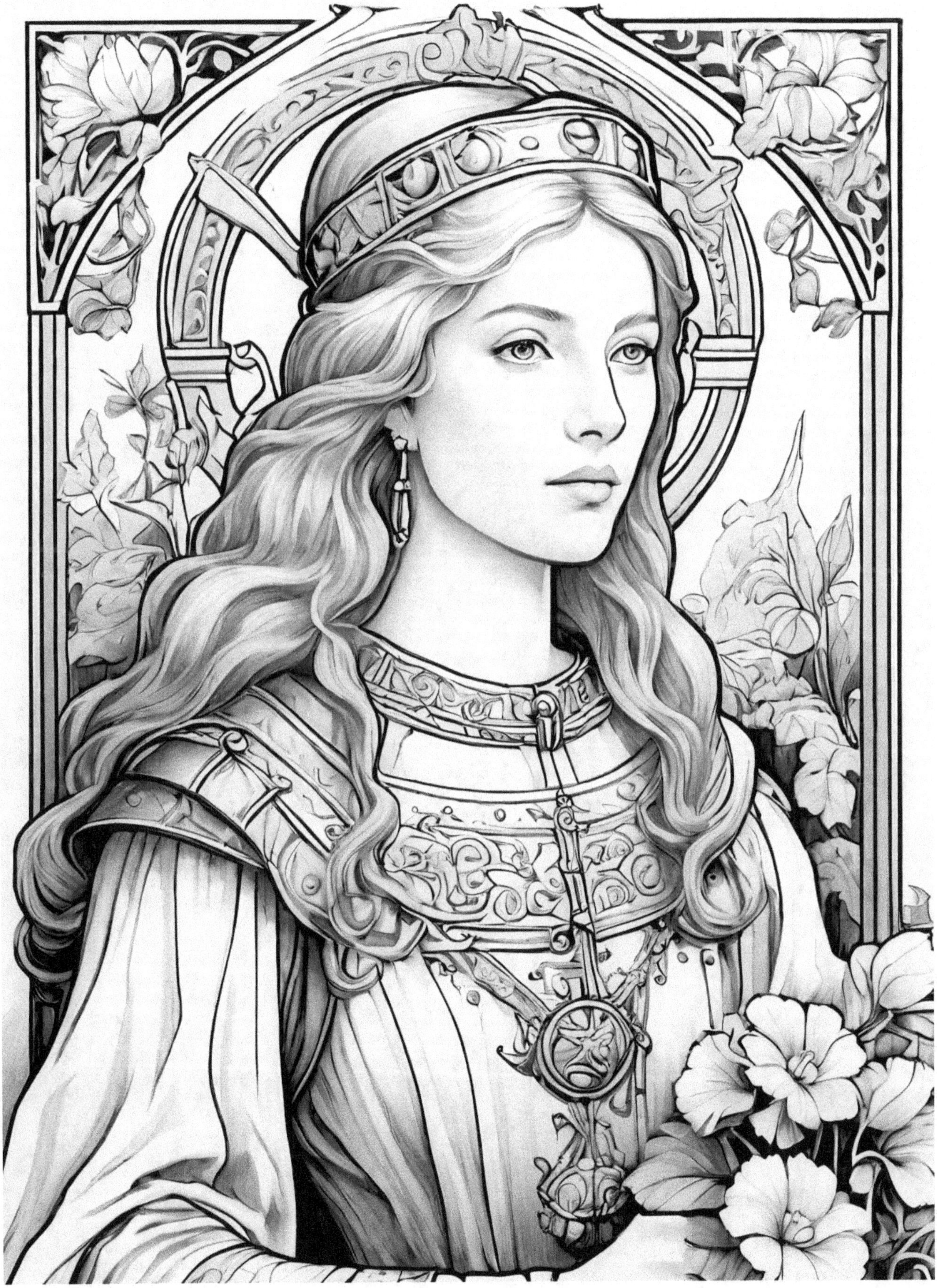

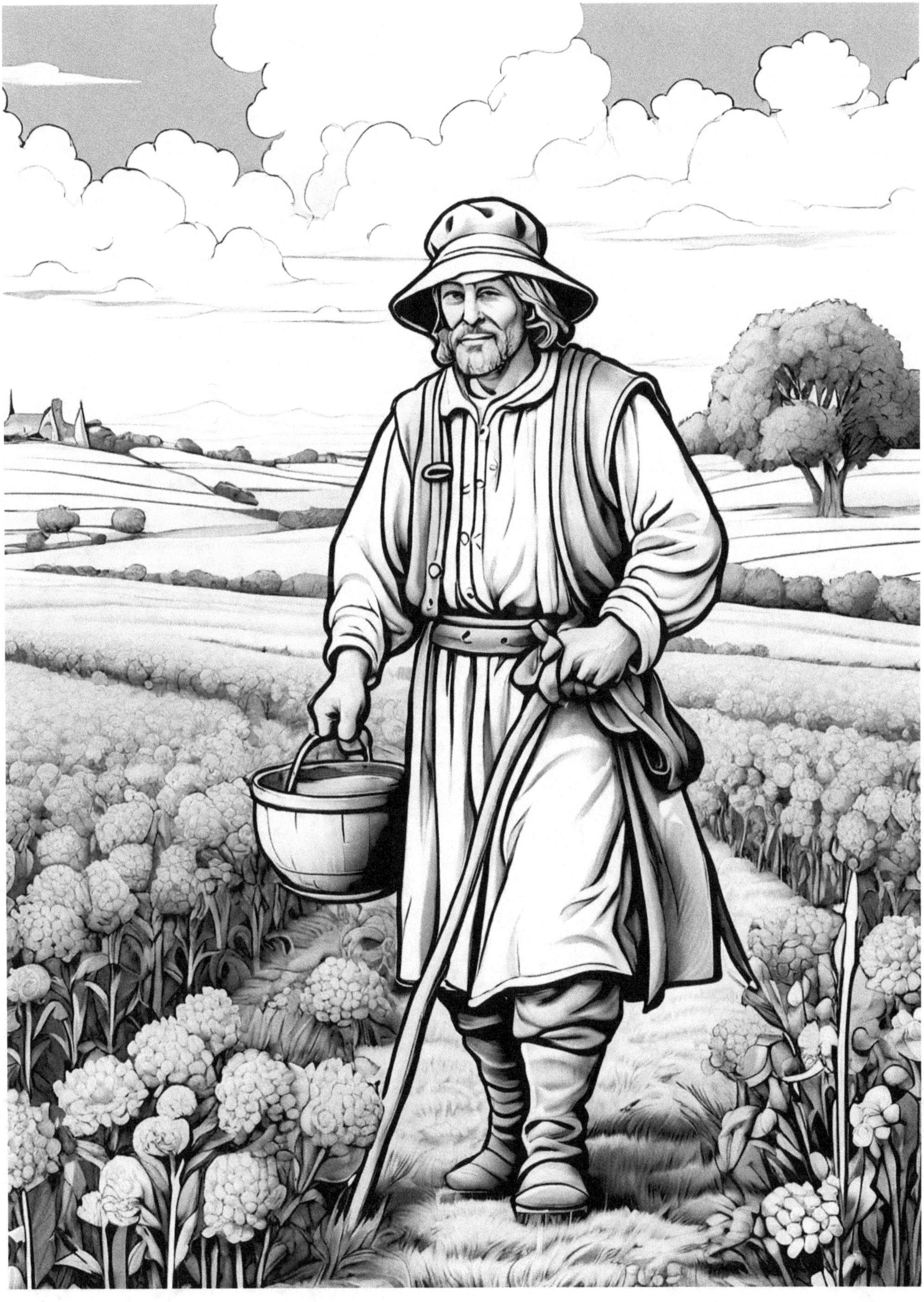

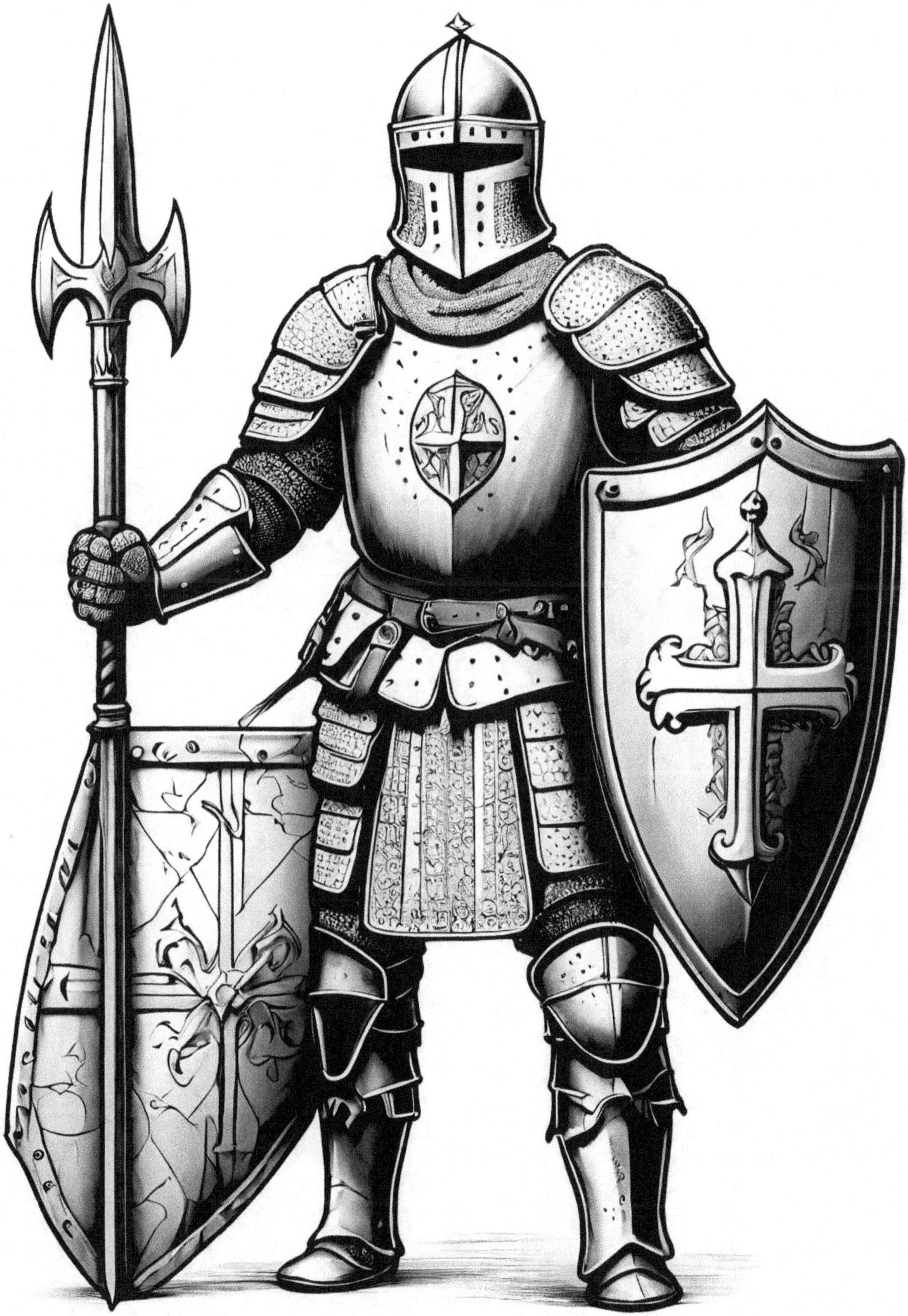

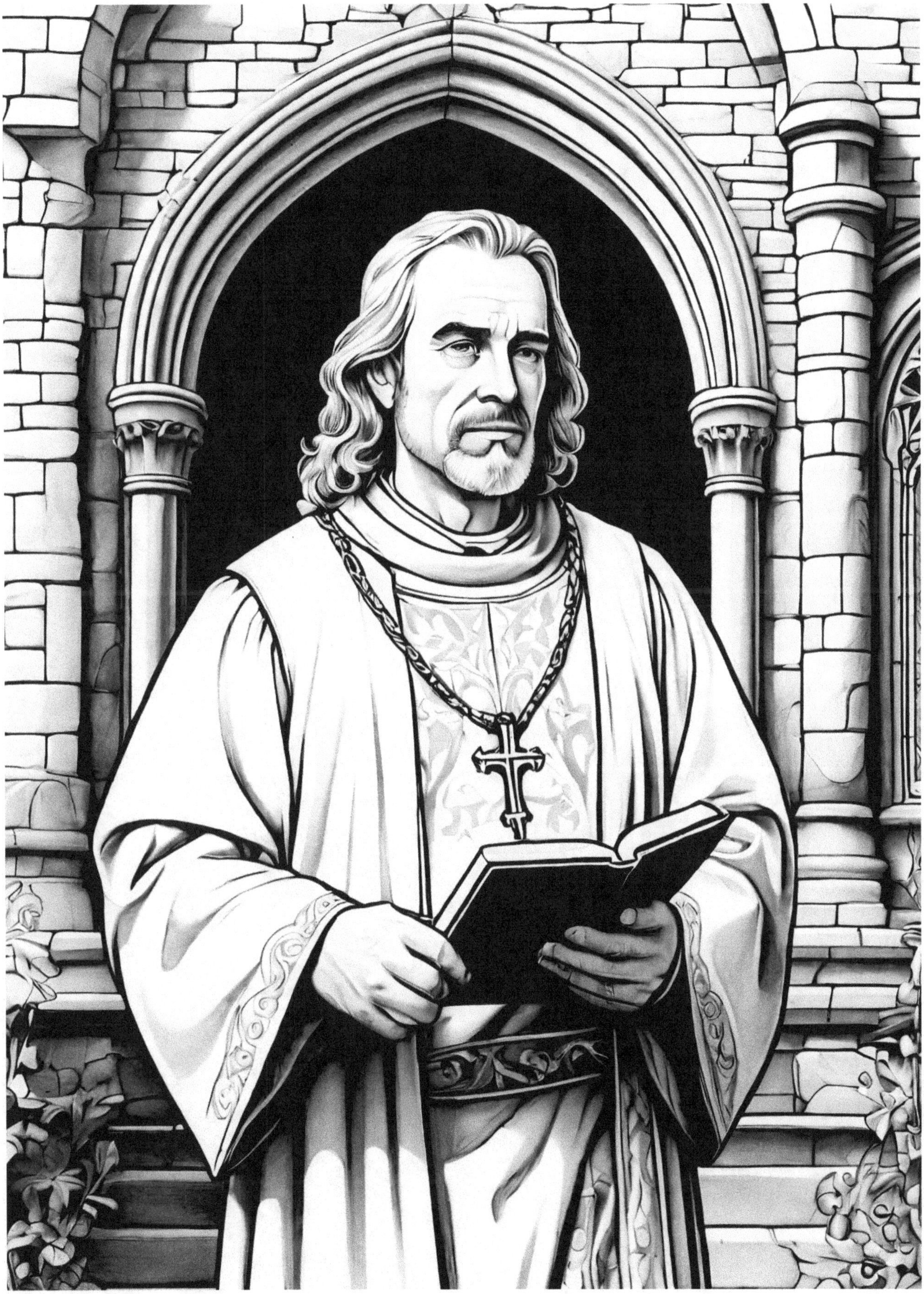

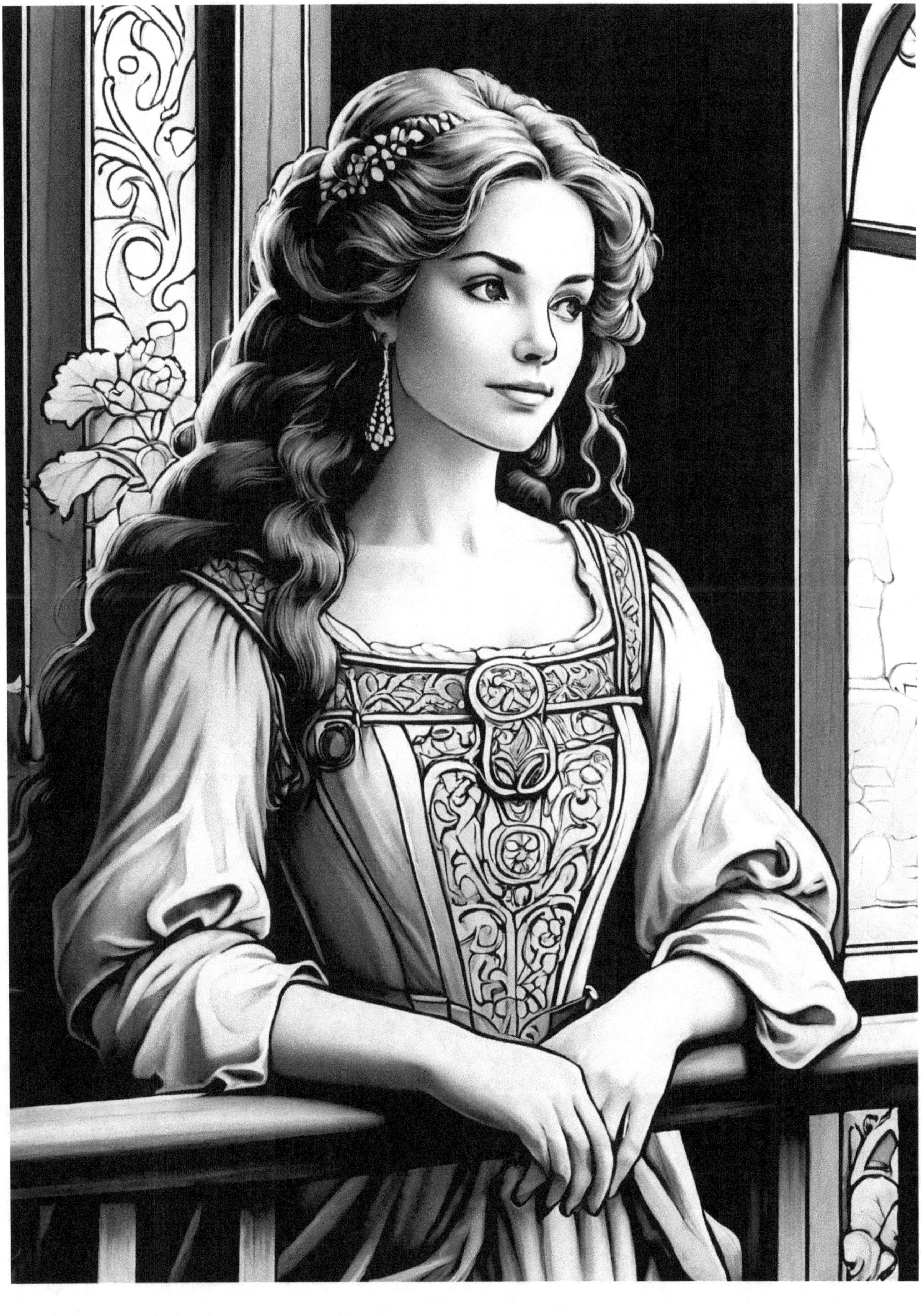

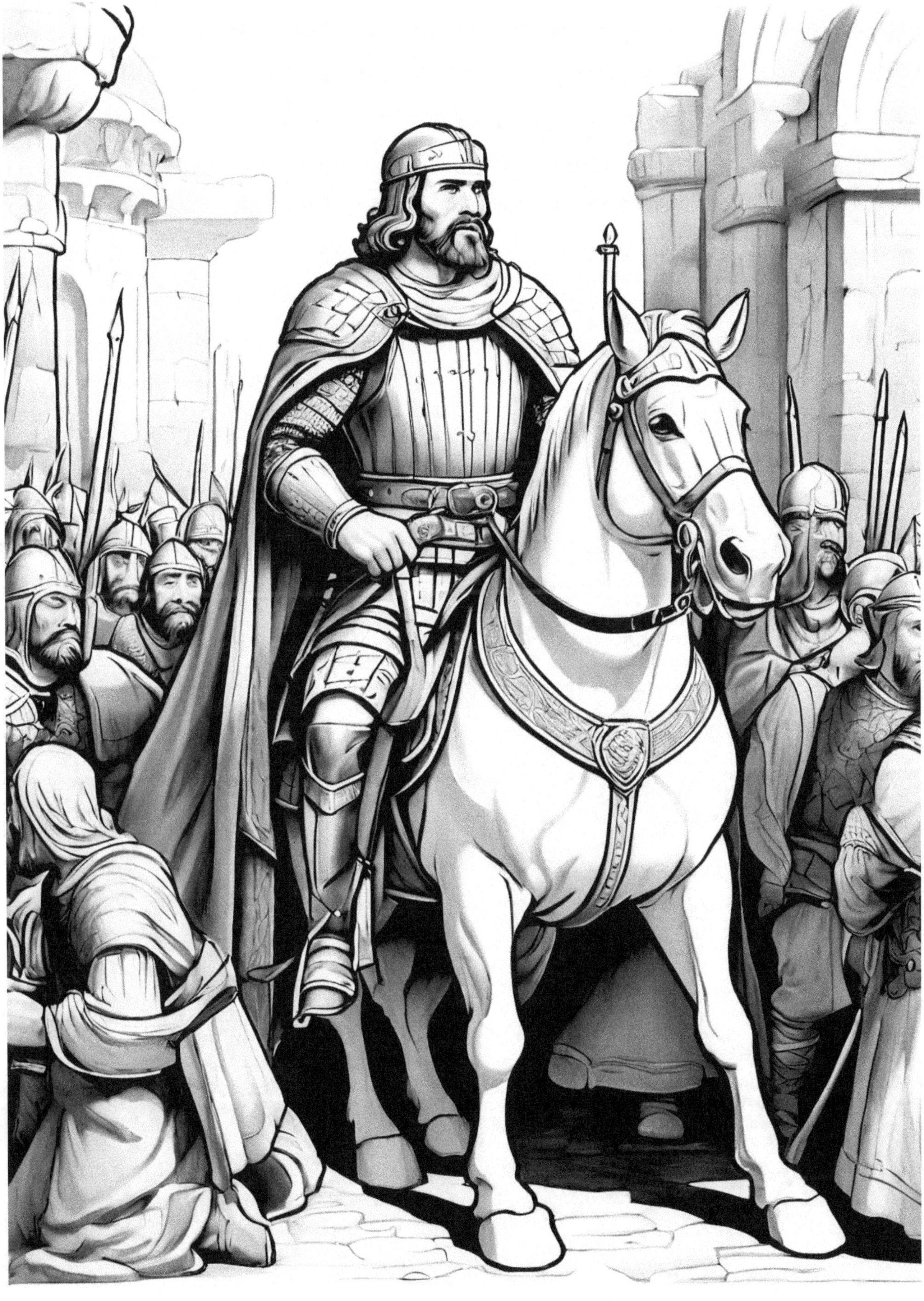

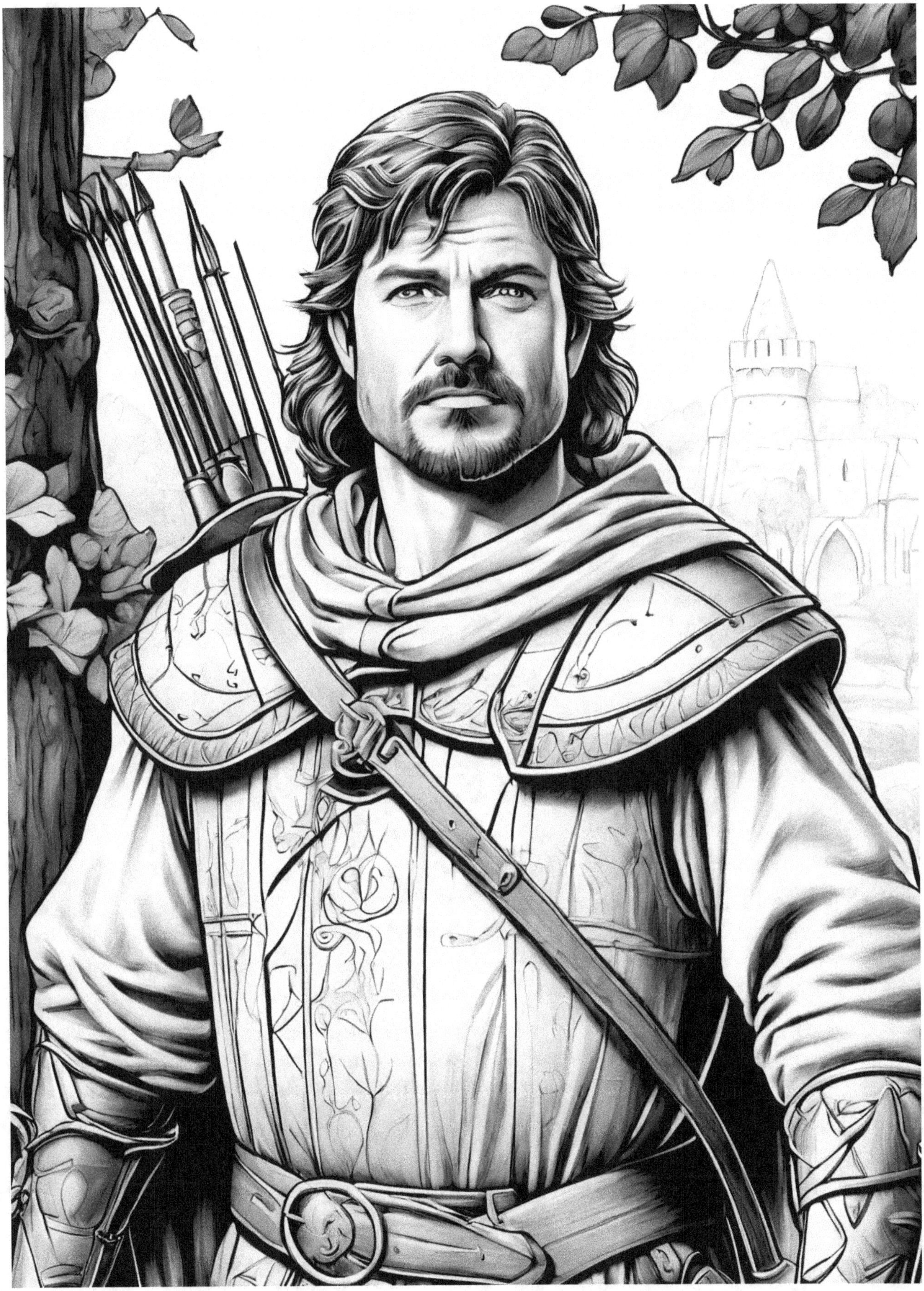

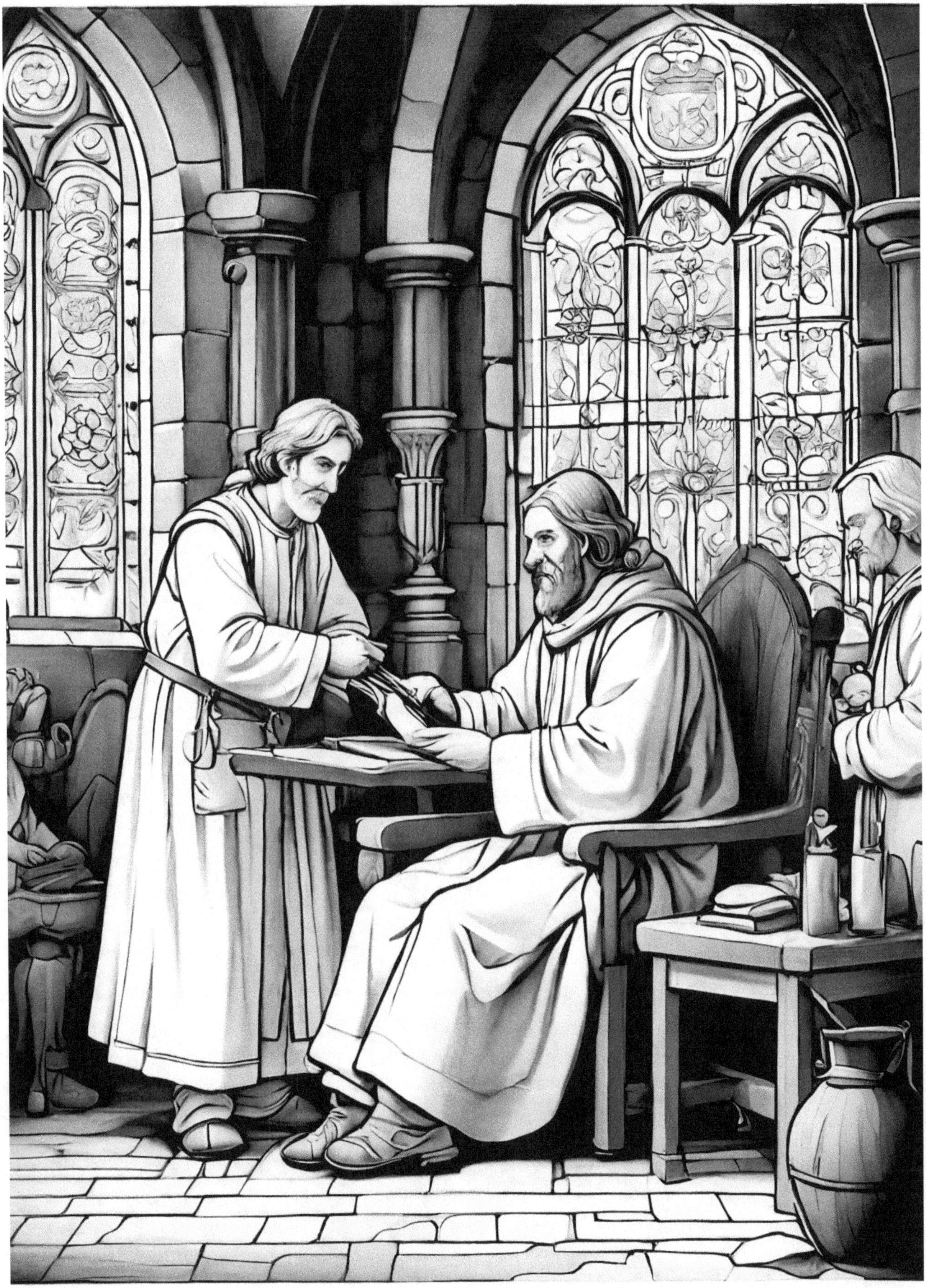

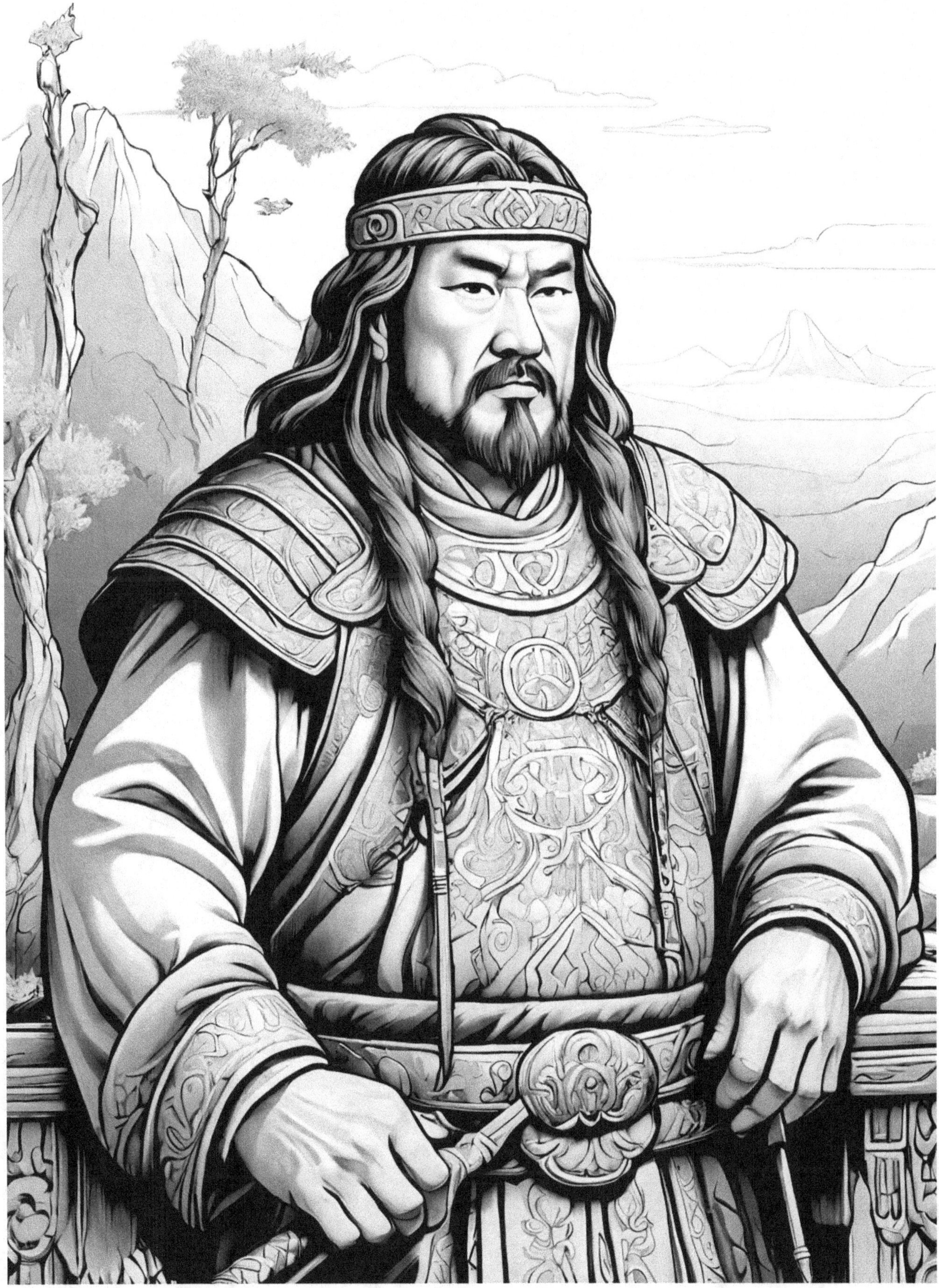

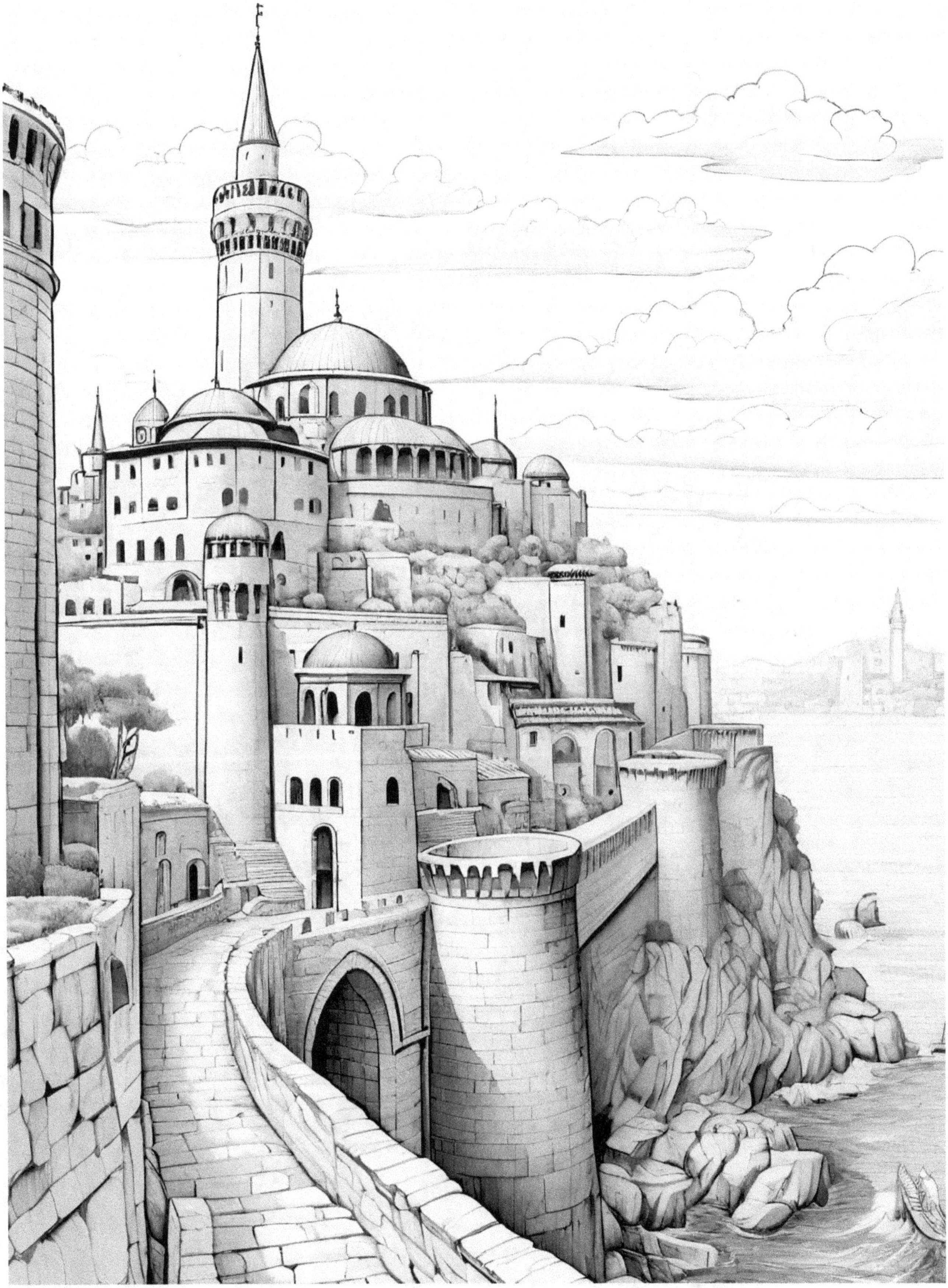

www.ingramcontent.com/pod-product-compliance
Lightning Source LLC
Chambersburg PA
CBHW081003290526
45795CB00009B/3062
* 9 7 9 8 8 7 8 8 0 3 2 2 9 *